U0065147

For my father, Stanley Golembe,
who first took me to the circus

ZIPPY AND THE CIRCUS

by Carla Golembe

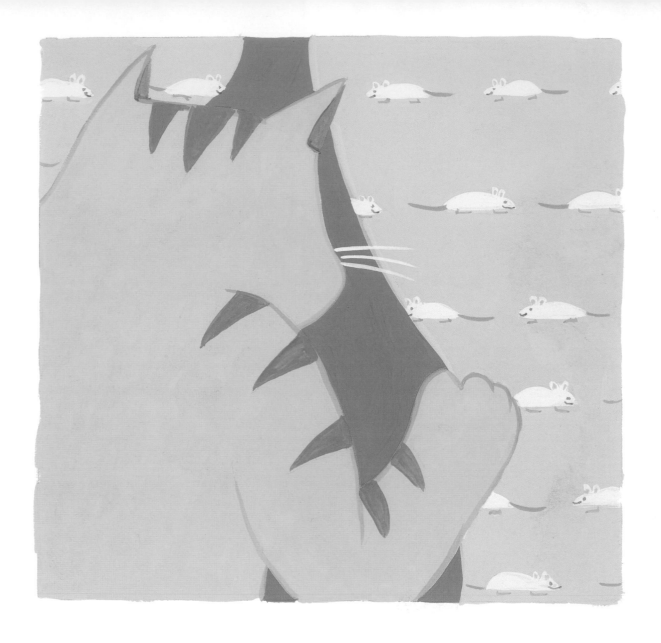

One morning Zippy hears music. He looks out of the window.

People and animals are dancing in the street. They are *dressed up for a *celebration.

There are horses and elephants.

There are other animals ringing bells.

There are people playing drums and wearing masks.

Zippy is so interested he jumps out of the window.

He dances down the street and follows the *parade.

He follows them to a tent.

Zippy goes inside.

He looks around the tent and can't believe his eyes.

In the center of the tent is a circle of light.

Inside the circle is a VERY big cat.

This cat has *stripes just like Zippy.

This cat has green eyes, just like Zippy.

This cat has *whiskers just like Zippy. But, Zippy thinks, this cat is *as tall as a house!

A woman is holding a *hoop and the big cat jumps through it.

Zippy is so excited that he tries to follow the big cat through the hoop. He falls down. He *lands on his tummy.

The big cat shakes her head. She jumps through the hoop.
She makes it look easy to do.

"MEOW," cries Zippy. He tries again.

This time when he follows the big cat he seems to fly.

He lands on her back and *takes a bow.

The people love it! They clap their hands. They *shout, "What a clever cat!"

When Zippy gets home, he is so tired he goes right to sleep.
He doesn't even call Zoe.

But the next morning, *as soon as the sun comes up, Zoe calls
Zippy on the phone.
"Your picture is in today's newspaper," she tells him.

And there, on the *front page, is a picture of Zippy and the very big cat.

生字表

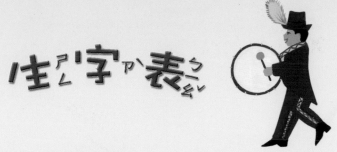

circus [ˋsɝkəs] n. 馬戲團

n.= 名詞，v.= 動詞

賽ㄙㄞˋ皮ㄆㄧˊ與ㄩˇ馬ㄇㄚˇ戲ㄒㄧˋ團ㄊㄨㄢˊ

⭐ *p.2*

有ㄧㄡˇ天ㄊㄧㄢ早ㄗㄠˇ上ㄕㄤ，賽ㄙㄞˋ皮ㄆㄧˊ聽ㄊㄧㄥ到ㄉㄠˋ一ㄧ陣ㄓㄣˋ音ㄧㄣ樂ㄩㄝˋ聲ㄕㄥ。他ㄊㄚ往ㄨㄤˇ窗ㄔㄨㄤ外ㄨㄞˋ看ㄎㄢˋ了ㄌㄜ看ㄎㄢˋ。

⭐ *p.3*

有ㄧㄡˇ一ㄧ群ㄑㄩㄣˊ人ㄖㄣˊ和ㄏㄜˊ動ㄉㄨㄥˋ物ㄨˋ在ㄗㄞˋ街ㄐㄧㄝ道ㄉㄠˋ上ㄕㄤ跳ㄊㄧㄠˋ舞ㄨˇ，他ㄊㄚ們ㄇㄣ全ㄑㄩㄢˊ都ㄉㄡ為ㄨㄟˋ了ㄌㄜ慶ㄑㄧㄥˋ祝ㄓㄨˋ活ㄏㄨㄛˊ動ㄉㄨㄥˋ而ㄦˊ盛ㄕㄥˋ裝ㄓㄨㄤ打ㄉㄚˇ扮ㄅㄢˋ。

⭐ *p.4-5*

其ㄑㄧˊ中ㄓㄨㄥ有ㄧㄡˇ馬ㄇㄚˇ兒ㄦˊ和ㄏㄜˊ大ㄉㄚˋ象ㄒㄧㄤˋ，有ㄧㄡˇ其ㄑㄧˊ他ㄊㄚ搖ㄧㄠˊ著ㄓㄜ鈴ㄌㄧㄥˊ的ㄉㄜ動ㄉㄨㄥˋ物ㄨˋ們ㄇㄣ，有ㄧㄡˇ人ㄖㄣˊ在ㄗㄞˋ打ㄉㄚˇ鼓ㄍㄨˇ，有ㄧㄡˇ人ㄖㄣˊ戴ㄉㄞˋ著ㄓㄜ面ㄇㄧㄢˋ具ㄐㄩˋ。

⭐ *p.6*

賽ㄙㄞˋ皮ㄆㄧˊ非ㄈㄟ常ㄔㄤˊ感ㄍㄢˇ興ㄒㄧㄥˋ趣ㄑㄩˋ，所ㄙㄨㄛˇ以ㄧˇ他ㄊㄚ跳ㄊㄧㄠˋ出ㄔㄨ窗ㄔㄨㄤ外ㄨㄞˋ。

⭐ *p.7*

他ㄊㄚ在ㄗㄞˋ街ㄐㄧㄝ道ㄉㄠˋ上ㄕㄤ一ㄧ路ㄌㄨˋ跳ㄊㄧㄠˋ著ㄓㄜ舞ㄨˇ，跟ㄍㄣ隨ㄙㄨㄟˊ著ㄓㄜ遊ㄧㄡˊ行ㄒㄧㄥˊ的ㄉㄜ隊ㄉㄨㄟˋ伍ㄨˇ。

⭐ *p.8*

他ㄊㄚ跟ㄍㄣ著ㄓㄜ他ㄊㄚ們ㄇㄣ來ㄌㄞˊ到ㄉㄠˋ一ㄧ個ㄍㄜˋ帳ㄓㄤˋ篷ㄆㄥˊ。

⭐ *p.9*

賽ㄙㄞˋ皮ㄆㄧˊ走ㄗㄡˇ了ㄌㄜ進ㄐㄧㄣˋ去ㄑㄩˋ。

⭐ *p.10*

他看看帳篷四周，簡直不敢相信他的眼睛！
在帳篷的中央打了一道聚光。
在聚光燈下，有一隻超級大貓。

✿ *p.11*

這隻貓身上的斑紋，跟賽皮的好像。

⭐ *p.12*

牠的綠色眼睛，跟賽皮的也很像。

✿ *p.13*

牠還有跟賽皮一樣的鬍鬚。可是，賽皮覺得，
這隻貓就像房子一樣高！

⭐ *p.14*

有個女人手上拿著一個圈圈，這隻大貓穿越圈
圈中間跳了過去。

✿ *p.15*

賽皮非常興奮，他試著要跟隨大貓穿越圈圈，
可是他跌倒了，肚子著地。

⭐ *p.16*

大貓搖了搖頭。她又穿越圈圈跳了過去，一副
很輕鬆的樣子。

⭐ *p.17*

賽皮大叫:「喵！」然後，他再試一次。這一次，他跟著大貓穿越圈圈的時候，好像飛了起來！

⭐ *p.18*

他降落在大貓的背上，鞠了一個躬。

⭐ *p.19*

大家都好喜歡賽皮的表演！他們鼓掌大喊:「好聰明的貓！」

⭐ *p.20*

當賽皮回到家時，他簡直累壞了，直接倒頭大睡，也沒有打電話給柔依。

⭐ *p.21*

但是隔天早上，太陽一升起來，柔依馬上打電話給賽皮。她告訴賽皮:「今天的報紙上，有你的照片呢！」

⭐ *p.22*

的確，就在頭版上，有一張賽皮與超級大貓的照片。

認識馬戲團

小朋友，你曾經看過馬戲團的表演嗎？如果有，什麼樣的表演讓你印象最深刻呢？請跟著一起做下面的練習，讓我們來認識馬戲團吧！

Part. 1

請聽 CD 的 Track 4，唸出這些有關馬戲團的英文單字：

circus tent
馬戲團帳棚

horse
馬

acrobat
特技演員

tiger
老虎

elephant
大象

animal trainer
馴獸師

27

Part. 2 下ㄒㄧㄚˋ面ㄇㄧㄢˋ這ㄓㄜˋ篇ㄆㄧㄢ文ㄨㄣˊ章ㄓㄤ，是ㄕˋ柔ㄖㄡˊ依一在ㄗㄞˋ報ㄅㄠˋ紙ㄓˇ上ㄕㄤˋ看ㄎㄢˋ到ㄉㄠˋ賽ㄙㄞˋ皮ㄆㄧˊ在ㄗㄞˋ馬ㄇㄚˇ戲ㄒㄧˋ團ㄊㄨㄢ歷ㄌㄧˋ險ㄒㄧㄢˇ的ㄉㄜ˙新ㄒㄧㄣ聞ㄨㄣˊ報ㄅㄠˋ導ㄉㄠˇ。請ㄑㄧㄥˇ根ㄍㄣ據ㄐㄩˋ第ㄉㄧˋ27頁ㄧㄝˋ的ㄉㄜ˙英ㄧㄥ文ㄨㄣˊ單ㄉㄢ字ㄗˋ和ㄏㄢˋ下ㄒㄧㄚˋ面ㄇㄧㄢˋ的ㄉㄜ˙提ㄊㄧˊ示ㄕˋ圖ㄊㄨˊ，圈ㄑㄩㄢ出ㄔㄨ正ㄓㄥˋ確ㄑㄩㄝˋ的ㄉㄜ˙單ㄉㄢ字ㄗˋ。（正ㄓㄥˋ確ㄑㄩㄝˋ答ㄉㄚˊ案ㄢˋ在ㄗㄞˋ第ㄉㄧˋ29頁ㄧㄝˋ喔ㄛ！）

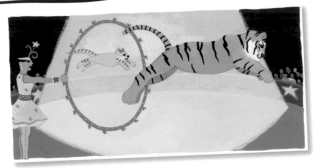

Cat Times

Zippy the cat performed in a circus yesterday. Yesterday morning Zippy heard music. He saw **(animal trainers/ acrobats)** and **(an elephant/a horse)** in the street. He was so interested that he followed the parade. In the center of a tent Zippy found a VERY big cat—it's a **(horse/ tiger)**! She jumped through a hoop and Zippy jumped through the hoop too! Zippy landed on the big cat's back and took a bow. The people were happy and said, "What a clever cat!"

雜技演員、一隻大象、老虎：

acrobats, an elephant, tiger

Zippy likes to jump. He jumps onto the chair. He jumps from the chair to the table. He jumps from the table to the couch. Sometimes he even jumps to the top of the refrigerator.

I love the circus. When I see Zippy jump I think he looks like a "Circus Cat."

作者的話

賽皮喜歡跳上跳下，他會跳到椅子上，然後從椅子上跳到桌上，最後再從桌上跳到沙發上。有時候，他甚至會跳到冰箱上面去呢！

我很喜歡馬戲團。當我看到賽皮跳來跳去的時候，我覺得他看起來就像隻「馬戲團的貓」。

🐾 About the Author

Carla Golembe is the illustrator of thirteen children's books, five of which she wrote. Carla has won several awards including a New York Times Best Illustrated Picture Book Award. She has also received illustration awards from Parents' Choice and the American Folklore Society. She has twenty-five years of college teaching experience and, for the last thirteen years, has given speaker presentations and workshops to elementary schools. She lives in Southeast Florida, with her husband Joe and her cats Zippy and Zoe.

🐾 關於作者

Carla Golembe 擔任過十三本童書的繪者，其中五本是由她寫作的。Carla 曾多次獲獎，包括《紐約時報》最佳圖畫書獎。她也曾獲全美父母首選基金會，以及美國民俗學會的插畫獎項。她有二十五年的大學教學經驗，而在過去的十三年中，曾經在多所小學中演講及舉辦研討會。她目前和丈夫 Joe 以及她的貓——賽皮與柔依，住在美國佛羅里達州東南部。

賽皮與柔依系列

ZIPPY AND ZOE SERIES

想知道我們發生了什麼驚奇又爆笑的事嗎？
歡迎學習英文0-2年的小朋友一起來分享我們的故事 ──
「賽皮與柔依系列」，讓你在一連串有趣的事情中學英文！

精裝／附中英雙語朗讀CD／全套六本

Carla Golembe 著／繪

本局編輯部 譯

Hello！我是賽皮，我喜歡畫畫、做餅乾，還有跟柔依一起去海邊玩。偷偷告訴你們一個秘密：我在馬戲團表演過喔！

Hi，我是柔依，今年最開心的事，就是賽皮送我一張他親手畫的生日卡片！賽皮是我最要好的朋友，他很聰明也很可愛，我們兩個常常一起出去玩！

賽皮與柔依系列有：

1 賽皮與綠色顏料
(Zippy and the Green Paint)
2 賽皮與馬戲團
(Zippy and the Circus)
3 賽皮與超級大餅乾
(Zippy and the Very Big Cookie)
4 賽皮做運動
(Zippy Chooses a Sport)
5 賽皮學認字
(Zippy Reads)
6 賽皮與柔依去海邊
(Zippy and Zoe Go to the Beach)

國家圖書館出版品預行編目資料

Zippy and the Circus:賽皮與馬戲團 / Carla
  Golembe 著;Carla Golembe 繪;本局編輯部譯.－
  －初版一刷.－－臺北市:三民,2006
    面; 公分.－－(Fun心讀雙語叢書.賽皮與柔
    依系列)
  中英對照
  ISBN 957－14－4451－0 (精裝)
  1.英國語言－讀本
523.38   94026565

網路書店位址 http://www.sanmin.com.tw

© Zippy and the Circus
—— 賽皮與馬戲團

著作人	Carla Golembe
繪 者	Carla Golembe
譯 者	本局編輯部
發行人	劉振強
著作財產權人	三民書局股份有限公司 臺北市復興北路386號
發行所	三民書局股份有限公司 地址／臺北市復興北路386號 電話／(02)25006600 郵撥／0009998－5
印刷所	三民書局股份有限公司
門市部	復北店／臺北市復興北路386號 重南店／臺北市重慶南路一段61號
初版一刷	2006年1月
編 號	S 806181
定 價	新臺幣壹佰捌拾元整

行政院新聞局登記證局版臺業字第○二○○號

有著作權·不准侵害

ISBN 957－14－4451－0 (精裝)